Knowledge Is Power

Lessons to Become a Successful Union Steward

By Jon Voss

DORRANCE
PUBLISHING CO
EST. 1920
PITTSBURGH, PENNSYLVANIA 15238

Dorrance Publishing Co
585 Alpha Drive
Pittsburgh, PA 15238
Visit our website at *www.dorrancebookstore.com*

ISBN: 979-8-88812-257-0
eISBN: 979-8-88812-757-5

Written with respect to all lives lost as a result of their labor. And in loving
memory of unionist, Richard McCabe.
Solidarity forever.
May you all rest in power.

You've just been chosen, elected, or appointed to be the union steward at your workplace. And just as quickly as you've received many congratulations, you're now assigned with a new set of challenging tasks... Or maybe you're an experienced steward looking to refine your already existing skills. Regardless of your steward experience or lack thereof, this book will provide you guidance to help you become more successful.

Being a union steward is an essential role, and many stewards are thrown right into the fire with little or no training. Simultaneously, an expectation of perfection from your members is almost immediate. This is normal, don't beat yourself up over the steep learning curve that comes with your new role, or your inability to immediately grasp and master all nuances related to the role. While being a union steward can at times be one of the most thankless jobs in the labor movement, it is vitally important and an enormous responsibility.

So, why did you become a steward? You became a steward because you believe no hard-working American should receive anything less than the best from their employer. Yet, you understand that many workers, even unionized workers, work day-in and day-out with little to no respected for their labor. This is where you, a steward, are needed most.

As a steward you have the legal authority to address the concerns of your members and can stand toe-to-toe with management when in a representative role. To successfully fulfill the role of a steward, you must accept the responsibility to demand what's right, what's fair, and what's reasonable for your members and you must dedicate yourself to achieving their desired outcomes.

As you begin to represent your members, you'll be provided opportunities to improve lives and communities, but you should also prepare yourself for impossible tasks, painful losses, and many difficult, heartfelt conversations.

You may have been a crucial member before you transitioned to being a steward but you now must accept the responsibility of dedicating yourself to your members and devote your time to their concerns.

To achieve this, most stewards establish their own methods of handling workplace issues in what is commonly referred to as a steward's "tool bag." This book, written in similar fashion to how many union contracts are written, contains resources and tips for you to add to your "tool bag" to help you become a successful union steward.

Just as many union contracts have articles or provisions that are supported by other parts of the contract, this book will reference itself for supporting information. Ideally, you should view this as more of a compass than an immediate answer to all your representational needs. When you think of a compass, does it tell you exactly how to get from point-a to point-b, or does it show you the direction you're traveling while trying to get to your destination? If you're unaware of how a compass works, the answer is the latter. The compass does not tell you how to get where you want to go but it can help guide you along your way. Use this book as a compass on your new journey.

Here's your first tip: expect little praise from what will hopefully become a career of successful interactions you have representing the interests of your members.

Are you ready?

Table of Contents

Article One – Unity Is Your Strongest Power   **1**

1.1 – Building Solidarity   2

1.2 – Bridge Trusting Relationships   3

1.3 – Loss Prevention   5

Article One Scenario   6

Article One Summary   7

Article Two – The Importance Of Respect   **9**

2.1 – Showing Respect   10

2.2 – Respecting Your Manager   11

2.3 – Difficult Managers   13

2.4 – Know Your Enemy   14

2.5 – Be Understanding   15

2.6 – Respectfully Disagree   16

2.7 – Focus On The Task At Hand   17

Article Two Scenario   18

Article Two Summary   19

Article Three – Grievances And Your Legal Authority   **21**

3.1 – Filing A Grievance   22

3.2 – Making Your Members Whole   23

3.3 – Past Practices   24

3.4 – Including But Not Limited To   25

3.5 – The Seven Steps Of Just Cause   25

3.6 – Protective Status   27

Article Three Scenario   28

Article Three Summary   29

Table of Contents

Article Four – Investigations And Documentation 31

4.1 – Perform Your Own Investigation 31

4.2 – The 'E' In E-Mail 32

4.3 – Who, What, When, Where, Why, And How 33

4.4 – Hidden Reasons 35

Article Four Scenario 36

Article Four Summary 38

Article Five – References And Resources 39

5.1 – Weingarten Rights 39

5.2 – Laws Pertaining To Labor 40

5.3 – Government Organizations 43

5.4 – Non-Government Organizations 44

Article Five Summary 46

Article Six – Bargaining > Arguing 47

6.1 – Member vs. Member 48

6.2 – Member vs. Manager 49

6.3 – Working To The Rule 50

Article Six Summary 52

In Closing 53

Article One

<u>Unity</u> Is Your Strongest Power

It is vital that you and your members are on the same page and present a unified front to all workplace issues. The more united you and your shop siblings are, the less likely a manager will treat you inhumanely, the less likely they are to violate your contractual rights, and its less likely that they'll attempt to unreasonably reprimand one of your members.

Never forget, as a union worker you have rights on the job. These rights were won by those who came before you. Rights are never given; every worker's rights and benefits were hard earned and are the direct result of previous workers' identifying and strategically fighting for workplace safety and security.

The benefits we enjoy today, especially those that followed many workplace injuries and on the job deaths that clearly identified a need for change required a battle with company bosses.

Every one of your worker rights can be lost and ignored if you don't demand they continue to be recognized. It is up to you to fight like hell to improve upon and keep existing rights and benefits.

Say it out loud: We as union workers have rights on the job!

As a steward, you have a lot of responsibilities, with many people counting on you to protect them and their livelihoods. How you carry out your duties is dependent on many influences including, but not limited to, contract language, laws, company rules, and regulations and you should be aware of all that apply to your specific situation.

Notwithstanding, one thing holds true no matter where you work and how you address your members' concerns, and that is _unity_. If you have an army of members standing with you while you engage management then you're 100% more likely to be successful in whatever issue you're addressing.

Now, _unity_ alone doesn't guarantee you'll be successful—you must still do everything in your power to deliver desired results to your members. The support of your members is key and elevating your members to stand in solidarity simply levels the playing field for you when you go to battle with management. So, at every opportunity, leverage scenarios of _unity_ to make your members whole.

You will read more information on making your members whole later... Right now, it's time to strengthen _unity_ among your members and unlock your true potential as a successful steward.

1.1 - Building Solidarity

How do you build solidarity among your members? To be honest, there is no one-size-fits-all in this scenario, but solidarity starts with you checking in on your members. Maybe hourly, daily, or weekly—determine what works best for you, just be consistent and do it as often as you can.

It is imperative that you gauge your members' _unity_ on a regular basis by engaging with them. This is especially true when you have new employees. And even more so if this is their first union represented job. At every opportunity, engage members in small-talk conversations reinforcing the idea that the "union" is here to help. Talk up the benefits you all have because of your union and how your life is better simply because of these benefits. Make the correlation that these benefits were earned by the membership working together. This is how you begin to build _unity._

On a regular basis, update your members on everything going on with the company as well as anything going on with your union. Strike up conversations about members' families, their goals, and their lives in general. Provide your members with union flyers, stickers, t-shirts, hats, etc., and start a solidarity day. A solidarity day can be as simple as everyone wearing the same union t-shirt every Tuesday, or everyone wearing a _unity_ button in support of a topic or grievance at work. Are wages low? Provide _unity_ buttons with creative wage related slogans for everyone to wear at work and whenever they're speaking to an agent of the company.

Example: "Currently working for less than I deserve", "Take this wage and SHOVE IT!", "Over worked and under paid."

When it comes to wearing _unity_ buttons, you are only limited to your own imagination. The goal is for your members to send a message to the company by speaking with one voice about a specific issue or topic. Power in numbers is the name of the game, and your message will speak louder when more and more of your members participate in a unified way.

When you start a _unity_ campaign or solidarity day, remember you cannot and should not coerce anyone to participate. Instead, you should lead your members by example and ask your strongest supporters to join you beforehand. If a large group of you walk into work one day wearing the same t-shirt or button, you'll likely have others that show interest and some who simply need to be asked to join the group. Be sure to bring enough for everyone and keep extras readily available.

Remember, your members must have absolute faith in you and your dedication. In their eyes, you are the union, and you must be equally beholden to them, as you are to union principles. In doing so, you'll build solidarity among your membership, and you'll become a better steward for your actions.

1.2 - Bridge Trusting Relationships

The motto 'under promise and over deliver' should become one you adhere closely to. The saying seems a bit corny and simplistic, but it works. Everyone is pleased when they receive more than they expect and you'll be better off if you temper expectations by under promising and over delivering.

Never promise an outcome and never lie to your members because your members need to know they can _trust_ you. You can easily lose someone's _trust_ if you promise an outcome you can't deliver, and you will quickly lose _trust_ if you're caught lying.

Avoid making promises generally, not just specific outcomes, because unexpected forces or even events outside of the workplace can derail the most perfect of grievances and your members will lose _trust_ in you if you're unable to deliver on the promises you made. Instead of promising, demonstrate that you take your member's concern seriously and that you're dedicated to working towards a positive result for them. Inform them that you'll leave no stone unturned, and you'll examine every ounce of detail pertinent to their case. Then do just that and follow up with the work you say you will do.

Additionally, you should never lie because you don't want your member to feel as if you don't value them enough to tell them the truth. Does the truth hurt? Yeah, sometimes it does. But losing your member's _trust_ is worse than telling them what they don't want to hear. So, be honest, open, and transparent. And, if applicable, have the hard conversation in a timely manner. This will build _trust_.

Note: If you're unable to deliver a desired outcome, you must own the outcome you get. Own up to your mistakes. Own the loss. Own everything. Remind your members that you'll never forget how the company treated them, and that you'll work even harder each time going forward.

So, what do you do if you know you're 100% correct about a specific grievance or violation? Remember to never promise, to never lie, and simply deliver the results you know your members deserve. Try challenging your members to participate in your grievances. Did your member witness something specific to the case? Or was a questionable interaction with management seen by others? By asking your members to get involved you'll make them feel as if they are a part of something bigger than themselves and when they see the results of their participation they will start to _trust_ you as their steward. They must feel this _trust_. Their participation is essential to building _unity_.

Building _trust_ can take a long time. To help, become the go-to-expert for everything. Admittedly, this is a challenge, so here's a _tip: you don't have to have all the answers, but you must be able to direct your members to someone who can adequately answer their questions._

Sometimes the best person is a benefits expert, chief shop steward, business representative, human resources, or even legal counsel, depending on the structure of your company and union organization. You should have a list of subject matter experts both within and outside of your union and you should utilize that list as necessary. As an example, you may have a new member who moved from out of state and they're looking for a reputable auto mechanic or want to know a safe place to buy a home—the possibilities are endless, as should your resources and contacts. Whatever the concern, make sure you listen and correctly direct them to the answer or appropriate resource. Build it and they will come, right? Becoming the go-to-expert will keep your members engaged and unified, justifying their belief that they can _trust_ you.

1.3 – Loss Prevention

There will come a time where you'll be the one to help a member in the event they're suffering from drugs and/or alcohol. So, obtain and retain contact information to a resource group (AA or whomever) and plan on attending a group meeting with your member whenever possible. Keep it in the back of your mind that you're not there because you can fix their problems, but that you're there because you care about their wellbeing, and you want them to _trust_ that you do. Remind them you care. Show them you care. Be there for them so they can feel appreciated while going through a difficult period.

Unfortunately, you may encounter a member with suicidal thoughts or desires and you may quickly become entangled in a situation where you need to get them the correct help they deserve. If you experience this, DO NOT panic. Take a mental step back and listen closely to what your member is saying. Remind them you care for them and want to introduce them to an expert. This is where you will need reliable contacts. DO NOT hesitate to make that call because it very well could be the call that saves someone's life.

Additionally, some states, union contracts and/or employers may have further obligations you should be aware of, and depending on where you live and work, you might be required to contact additional emergency services or follow a protocol for a de-escalation program. If this applies to you, follow this protocol as it's documented.

Time is of the essence anytime a member has suicidal ideations. So, whether you're obligated to or not, take the initiative and make the appropriate calls at the soonest opportunity because your member needs help.

Furthermore, many unions offer their own assistance programs, as do a lot of large employers. There are also government help lines and prevention groups available 24/7. So, know your area and the available resources for you to lean on. If you can, make personal contacts within these agencies before you need them and utilize them when you do need them.

Article One Scenario

A group of workers have been assigned to a new direct line supervisor. This supervisor believes in the failed tactics of yelling, bullying, and micromanaging. Without providing training or reason, the new supervisor assigns many new labor-intensive tasks to everyone and threatens to reprimand anyone who isn't working at a pace the supervisor believes is fair. If rushed, some of these tasks could cause bodily harm and this generates the opportunity to create a low-quality product. After a short period of time, the morale of your shop has dwindled, and your members are coming to you concerned about their livelihoods because the supervisor is threatening to fire anyone who challenges their authority. Additionally, many members are now experiencing shoulder pain from the repetitive tasks they're being bullied into doing at an unsafe rate.

What do you do?

Remember, *unity* is your strongest power and membership participation is key.

If you have the support of your members and they're willing to stand with you, then a federally protected action may be appropriate. A concerted activity, that is. Simply put, concerted activities are federally protected actions whenever a worker acts on behalf of their co-workers or when a group of workers act together to address workplace issues with their employer. Concerted activities can relate to, but are not limited to, wages, benefits, hours, and unsafe working conditions.

Do any ideas come to mind in how you can address the scenario above? Do you believe a group effort could help make changes? Imagine what would happen if you and your coworkers all came to work with one arm in a sling and you all inform the supervisor that the work they've been assigned and the rate of speed in which the supervisor expects the work to be performed at has now resulted in many work-related injuries. Do you think the supervisor would be forced to reevaluate? Do you think the company would appreciate a supervisor treating workers like this?

Not only do you have power in numbers, but you also increase your chances of success when dealing with an out-of-line supervisor—and it starts with *unity* among your membership.

Article One Summary

The most successful union stewards have the support of their members because their members know they can rely on the steward to deliver for them, and that you genuinely care for their wellbeing.

Your members must _trust_ you.
You must build _unity._
You must be honest, open, and transparent.
Be the go-to person for everything.
Never lie.
Never promise.
Deliver for your members.

unity: noun – the state of being united or joined as a whole.

trust: noun – a firm belief in the reliability, truth, ability or strength of someone or something.

Notes: ________________________________ ________________

____

____

____

____

____

____

____

Article Two

The Importance Of Respect

In order to become a successful union steward you must earn the _respect_ from, well, just about everyone. It is undoubtedly difficult to earn _respect_ and it can be burdensome if you are unsure how or unwilling to try but you can achieve it. You've probably heard the iconic phrase "_respect_ is earned, not granted" but have you ever sat down to evaluate how that applies to the role of being a shop steward?

A successful union steward understands that _respect_ is a deeply held emotion that can evaporate in the blink of an eye if they turn their back on anyone who respects them. So, always show _respect_, especially to those who don't necessarily _respect_ you. Yes, this is difficult, but you're not a steward because it's easy; you're a steward because you care about your members.

A failure to show _respect_ to others is a common mistake many people make when they're first elevated to a leadership role. Managers, CEOs, politicians, and other leaders all fall victim to this mindset, and so can a new steward. Don't deny yourself the opportunity to show your _respect_ to others because the ideal way to earn _respect_ is to give _respect_. So, you'll want to find ways to work with everyone, members, and management alike.

Think for a second, can you visualize someone who doesn't _respect_ others? Maybe a new manager who shows up and begins to lead-by-demand

and starts barking off orders? This is the same type of manager who believes their employees will work hard simply because they're instructed to do so. This rarely works in the manager's favor, and you don't want to succumb to the same fate as a bad manager. So, it's imperative you become a respectful person.

By showing a supporting and appropriate amount of _respect_ to others, you can introduce and, in time, instill your ideas and priorities into their mindset. No, this is not a magic trick and to be honest, some people are challenging to work with—no matter what, don't let their impossibility deter your efforts. Always be respectful.

2.1 - Showing Respect

Regardless of who you're talking with, a member, a manager, or the cashier at a convenience store near your workplace, treat them all with _respect_. Everyone deserves the same level of _respect_ from a union leader such as yourself and you can show that by being engaged in whatever topic or issue they're expressing when you speak to them.

One way to show _respect_ for others is to listen more, talk less and refrain from allowing distractions to interrupt engagements. Think about how you would feel if someone you were talking to stared off into the distance and looked at their phone or constantly glanced at their watch while you were trying to have a conversation with them. You would be unlikely to appreciate someone disinterested in your concerns, and you definitely wouldn't _respect_ them. So, don't allow yourself to be distracted while you're listening to others talk. Be engaged, be curious and listen to what they have to say because it's important to them.

As a sign of _respect_, whenever you're talking to someone or a group of people who might be irritated or angry, you'll want to ask open-ended questions and for clarifications. You should do this because it not only reinforces that you're listening but it also shows you want to be sure you follow the intent of what they're saying as well. Asking open-ended questions and giving the other person time to clarify specifics helps them feel the _respect_ you're giving them. If the person you're talking with is speaking too fast or repeatedly diverges from their issue, you'll need to redirect them to their own points. You can do this in many ways but try saying something to the effect of "I'm here for you and I care about your concerns. Please tell me exactly what's causing you to feel this way," then ask for a resolution they would ideally like to see. By doing this you give them a moment to collect their thoughts before conveying their message. Once they're clear about their needs, you can then ask for further supporting information and additional open-ended questions. Don't be alarmed if this tactic needs to be repeated, especially if someone is irate over a workplace issue.

Lastly, and simply put, there are basic things you can do to help show your _respect_ and they're as easy as opening and holding doors, offering to help carry objects, or making positive comments about someone's accomplishments. These are simple tasks you can follow and it's highly likely you already do these this on a regular basis, but if you put effort into doing this more often, people will ultimately _respect_ you and your role.

2.2 – Respecting Your Manager

One way to _respect_ your manager is to be willing to talk your manager up, give them compliments, educate them on things that "only you and your members know," "there are situations that only you, the steward, can address," and reinforce the idea that you're going to be the reason they're successful. This may sound counterproductive, but the importance of this communication is for the manager to feel as if you're both in this together, and that only together can you solve problems. Even if the manager causes more headaches than solutions, it's important for you to be able to work with them on behalf of your members.

To many managers, a union steward is a combatant, and in a sense they are right, but a successful steward can lead a manager to view them as a resource. To show your value as a resource, your actions must back up anything you say you'll address. Did you tell the manager you'd speak to a certain member about a specific issue? If so, make sure you speak to the member then follow up and let the manager know you've "handled the situation." The idea behind this is that you want to show the manager you are trustworthy and fulfilling an obligation to them is an ideal way to achieve this.

Another way of respecting your manager is to know where they come from, so ask them about their background, former places they lived or worked, their families, hobbies and what they might do if they won the lottery. Put effort into genuinely getting to know them. Do they have a preferred name or title they'd like you to use? Do they have a name or title they never want to hear again? Use the answers to both of those questions wisely. Are they former military? If so, thank them on a regular basis for their service to our country and ask if they are comfortable sharing stories about their experiences. You'll want to do these things because the more of a personable-working relationship you have with your manager the more likely they'll be willing to work with you at a time when you'll need it most.

Additionally, you've likely noticed most managers have a desk or office set up of some sort. When you're in or near their area, look around and see what they have on the walls, cubical, desk, etc., because many managers will give obvious clues about themselves to the entire world. Pictures alone should give you the ability to strike up many different conversations over a lengthy working relationship. This is a golden opportunity for you to learn, know and _respect_ who the manager is outside of work.

When you strike up conversations with your manager, keep the conversations about them and their interests. Be sure to ask open-ended and follow-up questions so they share in-depth details. When possible, relate to their answers, and address them by name. Just keep in mind that most people want to talk about themselves.

Example: New manager has pictures of themselves with people who appear to be their family, right? A couple kids, likely their spouse, the family dog, etc. And many pictures of what looks like a very fast boat where people are water-skiing.

Can you think of a situation where being knowledgeable about your manager could help you prevail in a disagreement? How do you think they'll treat your next grievance if you've shown you _respect_ them as a person? Might they react in a more lenient way, or do you think they'll hold back in negotiations? And can you relate to your manager while letting them do most of the talking? A respected person is more likely to be understanding and much easier to work with.

In these scenarios, it's completely acceptable to stretch the truth a little bit or rearrange your story to be more closely related to theirs so they too can relate. Just make sure you don't brazenly lie because you can lose all trust with the manager—remember the lesson from *Article 1.2* covering truth telling—it especially applies here.

You will become a successful steward when you and a manager can work hand-in-hand. The ultimate goal of showing _respect_ to your manager is to prevent an opportunity for them to take advantage of your members. If the manager notices you're there for more than simply being a check and balance on their management style, then you'll open doors where the manager becomes more lenient or is willing to "look the other way" on non-liability related issues. These doors are success stories for your members, and you first gain access to these doors by showing _respect_ for your manager.

Article 2.3 – Difficult Managers

No matter the industry you work in, management is pressured to have their employees properly achieve specific tasks. From manufacturing and agriculture to service work and hospitality, you name it, every manager's job relies on the work you and your members perform, or don't perform, and their success is directly correlated the success you and your members are set up to have.

Note: Your manager's job is incumbent on your labor. You should view this as potential leverage. A lever is how you move objects and leverage is how you move people. Use this information wisely.

So, how do you show _respect_ to a defiant or difficult manager? One thing you can do is remind them that you both have overlapping goals, though they might not realize it at first. If your manager lacks the ability to remove roadblocks or provide you the equipment needed to successfully execute your jobs, then the manager too will fail.

How would you evaluate a situation where the manager tells everyone to complete a set of tasks but doesn't provide them the necessary items, tools, or equipment to do their work? Remember, you need to show _respect_ to gain _respect_, and just as *Article 1.2* stated, you must be the go-to person for everything. Being the go-to person applies in this situation too. Can you think of a way to use your knowledge, along with your unified workforce, to leverage what you and your members need? Can you think of ways to motivate your difficult manager into becoming less difficult by showing them how successful or unsuccessful they can be through a show of force by you and your members?

Dealing with a difficult manager can take a lot of time, but you're destined to fail if you refuse to _respect_ the person you'd like them to be. In the event you find it hard to _respect_ them as a person, _respect_ their role, and use your unified leverage and attempt to morph them into the person your members deserve to report to.

2.4 - Know Your Enemy

By learning who your enemy is you can strategize the conversations and interactions you have with them when you're engaging in a representative manner, as your actions are directly related to your success.

So, who's the enemy? The enemy can be anyone from a direct line supervisor or someone within the multi-level management structure to the CEO, human resources professional, investors, company PR team, corporate influencers, or legal department, and it's beneficial for you to know who they are and to _respect_ them if you interact with them. To be clear, you may not _respect_ them because they're deserving of it (in many cases they are not) but you show you have _respect_ for them because their position within the company can have direct impacts to your members.

Once you learn who the enemy is, never stop learning about them. Understand their likes, dislikes, body-postering, slogans they use, celebrity affiliations, favorite or least favorite sports teams and players, politicians, etc. This can apply to any or all appreciations they might hold, but to be specific, if your enemy is a devoted fan of a certain athlete, then you should study this athlete. Learn some stats, memorize their character traits, charity affiliations, and focus on their greatest achievements and losses. Why? Because the enemy already has this information ingrained into their memory and their feelings of specific events will force them to react differently if and how you reference those events. By linking a scenario of one of your members to their favorite athlete, the enemy will instinctively evaluate the conversation differently. Use their personal preferences to your advantage whenever you need them to see things your way.

2.5 - Be Understanding

It's imperative you fully understand what it is the boss needs and you'll need to view it from their perspective. Once you see it from their angle, you can sway the topic in your desired path. Inform the boss that "you both have the same priorities", that you're "here to work with them, not against them" and want to "see the team be successful." You don't necessarily need to use those words but make the effort to arrange your conversations about the boss's needs and priorities, and the success your members could deliver if the boss chooses to work with them.

It's very easy in highly stressful jobs to have the desire to take on your boss "guns a blazing," and think you'll get a point across by "kicking ass and taking names." These methods can work but they fail more often than not. You cannot simply run into the boss's office and expect them to give a damn about anything you have to say until they feel there's a two-way-street of communication. If you feel like screaming at them, especially if you're 100% correct about whatever the topic is, remember to take a step back and give yourself sufficient time to collect your thoughts and talking points. Then, take a few deep breaths and walk to their office—don't run, walk. Walking gives you time to focus your attention and keeps your blood pressure down. Having elevated blood pressure makes it more difficult to remain calm during your conversation. So, take it slow and breathe.

It's crucial that you always keep your cool and refrain from using emotional outbursts. Think about the comment section of social media; where there are echo chambers of exclamation points, run on sentences, and unanswered questions. Speaking to the boss as if you're commenting on social media will result in nothing for you to brag about. Remaining in a calm and respectful, yet firm-toned voice, giving direct answers and asking specific questions will let the boss know you mean business and that you're also willing to give them an opportunity to reciprocate. This is where you'll achieve preferred results for your members. If and when the boss does not reciprocate your professional tone, change the subject, and deflect all conversations to something other than the initial topic at hand.

Example: A member gets into a heated argument with their boss and the boss now wants to "get into it" with you. To calm the situation try responding to them in the following: "Boss, today's been a highly stressful day, hasn't it? I blame this crazy weather we've been having... I honestly believe this heat is exacerbating everyone's emotional state, myself included. Let's table this conversation for now and reconvene once everything has cooled down."

Deflecting or changing the subject can sometimes be a great opportunity for your boss to relax over a recent event so you can hopefully have a better conversation at a later time. Sometimes it's an opportunity for them to vocally unload some stress or vent to you about unrelated events. Let them vent if they need. While they talk, use your body language to acknowledge whatever they're saying. If they're saying something good, then nod your head up and down and smile. If they're saying something negative then puff up your cheeks, grin a little and shake your head from side to side. If you don't instinctively replicate these bodily actions then practice your body language as an activity. Practice it alone, with a trusted confidant, in your car, at the grocery store, or in the mirror at the gym and imagine your bosses' comments when doing so. A successful steward will instinctively use their body language during a conversation, and as awkward as it can be, practicing body language will help you execute more naturally.

2.6 - Respectfully Disagree

Learning to keep your emotions in check and respectfully disagreeing can reward your opponent with a desire to work more closely with you during your next encounter. And in doing so, you'll begin to reach new levels of success. It's often necessary and perfectly okay to disagree. You can expect to do it a lot as a steward, but how you present yourself during a time of disagreement is how you set yourself up for success. In the future, you may look back and appreciate how you handled a disagreement because it'll lead to a later victory. Not all hills are worth dying on, and not every battle is a war defying moment, figuratively speaking.

When dealing with a member, a manager, the CEO, or a human resources expert, you need to recognize they all have varying opinions on every single issue under the face of the sun. No matter what your personal opinions are, be it religiously observant, politically viewed or a deeply held belief that you're unwilling to compromise on—keep them to yourself. Nothing you believe in is more relevant than the union principles that you must stand for when it comes to representing your members. Don't get caught up in a debate over the current culture war, and never argue about divisive topics. Stay laser focused on your members and deliver results for them.

Whenever possible, and as often as possible, let whomever you're dealing with know that you fully understand where they're coming from, that you see how sincere they are about whatever it is they believe, and that you _respect_ how they feel. People, more often than not, simply want to be heard and feel as if someone else is listening to them. Let them feel validated and move on with the conversation until you find an agreeing point. Once you find a mutually agreed point, bridge the conversation on from there and reinforce the agreed upon item. You can get more out of a conversation where both parties have some layers of agreement than from a conversation where you disagree about everything.

If and when you come to the end of conversation where you and the boss cannot agree on something specific, then reinforce the position that "you respectfully disagree" without giving any further justifying reasons. They've already dug their heels into their position, you've already spoken your piece; you'll be wasting time trying to change their mind. Instead, try to redirect the conversation or let them know you need to get back to work because "your work is important to the company's success." You won't be able to change their mind at this time, and any escalation will only cause harm to future engagements. The battle may have been lost but you have a workers' war to continue fighting so you'll have to find another way to achieve the results you're after.

If you have to agree to disagree in a conversation you're having with a member, then you'll need to make them feel as if they're not an outlier. To them, you are the union, and they can easily associate your personal beliefs as the official beliefs of your organization. So, try reminding them there are many other members who feel very similar to them and some who share the exact same feelings or beliefs. Your member needs to know you've still got their back no matter what you disagree on and that you _respect_ their position on the topic of discussion.

2.7 - Focus On the Task At Hand

Many in-person conversations end up like the comment section of a publicly available social media post, where people are shouting beliefs, making demands, attempting to tear down their opponent, and more often than not, no longer talking about the originating issue. In work related discussions, this is commonly referred to as "getting into the weeds" and is a tool to be used in your defense but it can also be used against your efforts.

If you find yourself in a conversation with management covering a pay dispute, for example, your manager might attempt to change the subject by making a comparison to another employee or a hypothetical situation having nothing to do with the pay dispute. When this happens, _respect_ the manager's words but don't let up on the pay dispute. You're there for your member and ending up in a conversation about an unrelated hypothetical situation is unlikely to have any positive impact on your need to deliver for them. When the conversation turns, try nodding your head in an appropriate direction while the manager talks and then increase the movement when you bring the conversation back to the original issue.

Remember, your primary concern is more important than any other topic your manager brings up, and you need to focus on getting a positive result for your member. So, don't get caught up in the weeds.

Article 2 - Scenario

Your members have concerns regarding a new work assignment they've been assigned because they don't have historical experience or training to help guide them and want you to talk to the manager on their behalf. Your manager is a huge football fan and follows the college he attended and played as a quarterback during a record winning season in the 2004-2005 school year. During your conversation, you inform the manager that your members are dedicated to completing the work but need help getting the tools they need to perform the job on time and with the highest of quality. Initially the manager is somewhat receptive but repeatedly reminds you how important it is to complete this work on time. So, you reinforce the dedication your members have to the work package as if they're the offense line protecting the quarterback and say to the manager, "Our team is a group of great workers, just like the offensive line of a great football team. If the offensive line doesn't have the training to protect the quarterback, then the quarterback isn't going to be successful. And I think we both know how important it is for a quarterback to be successful."

How do you think the manager will react after hearing you reference something he admires on a personal level? And can you see how this might lean the conversation in your direction?

Article Two Summary

The most successful union stewards have the ability to *respect* everyone they come in contact with, and this *respect* will open doors that lead to positive results for your members.

Show your *respect*.
Earn your *respect*.
Know who your enemies are and know who your friends are.
Learn to respectfully disagree.
Deliver for your members.

respect: noun – a feeling of deep admiration for someone or something elicited by their abilities, qualities, or achievements.

Notes: ____

____

____

____

____

____

____

Article Three

Grievances And Your Legal Authority

———

One of the pillars of being a successful union steward is to know what your legal authority is, how laws work in your favor, and how the law can work against you. Many companies spend large amounts of money on legal representation and provide training for managers and human resource professionals so they're aware of what legalities they must adhere to and which ones they can ignore. You read that correctly... many companies knowingly ignore some laws, rules, and regulations. Why? Well, you're better off asking them but most likely because they know they can get away with it or they are willing to pay the penalty for doing so. Knowing this, this is where a successful union steward can gain significant wins for their members, and it starts by knowing your legal authority.

First and foremost, you must know your union contract front to back, the organizational structure of your union and their preferred method of dealing with legal issues, discipline, terminations, and grievances. Most union contracts have language or a provision outlining the required steps to follow when dealing with workplace discrepancies. These steps are often based on geographical location, industry affiliations, business relations and other specifics that apply to, or are important to your union and your employer. I.e., the rules for a railway worker aren't necessarily the same for a restaurant worker and knowing the specifics that apply to your union is very important. So, learn who-is-who at your union and what the proper processes are so you can successfully execute your role as a steward.

Besides knowing your union contract from front to back, some general topics for you to think about would include, but are not limited to:

· What is your union structure when it comes to dealing with grievances? (Business Rep., Chief Shop Steward, Legal Counsel, Lodge President, etc.)
· What is the expectation of you as the steward?
· Do you have internal or external legal assistance?
· Must you approach your local lodge, or represented body before proceeding with a _grievance_?

Knowing the answers to these questions, and more, will help ensure you follow the necessary steps when filing a _grievance_ and will hopefully lead to a successful _grievance_. So, study your union structure as much as you study your union contract.

3.1 – Filing A Grievance

To understand a _grievance_, you must first understand what the order of events leading to a _grievance_ are. To grieve, or to file a _grievance_ is the legal procedure that follows an action or inaction taken by an employer against a union represented employee or group of employees. These actions or inactions can include, but are not limited to, violations of contractual obligations, non-compliance to state, federal, and/or local laws and regulations, past practices, arbitrational agreements, unreasonable disciplinary actions taken against a member, company policy violations and enforcement, and changes to working conditions.

The goal of the _grievance_ is to correct a violation or series of violations by making the effected member or members whole in all ways possible. A _grievance_ doesn't necessarily have to reach a high level of egregiousness to be worthy of review; it can be simple and to the point but be equally as important as a more complex _grievance_.

Example: A member being shorted one hour of overtime pay isn't necessarily egregious but it's definitely something to grieve. Whereas a member terminated *and mocked by their supervisor because of the member's religious beliefs would be egregious and is also something to be grieved.*

Many *grievances* can be handled before following with formal legal proceedings, depending on your union structure and the relationship you have with your company or manager or whoever you'll spend time with when addressing the issue presented to you by your member or members. So, make every effort to get a fitting agreement between yourself and the company before proceeding to a formal *grievance*.

There are times where the simple threat of a *grievance* works in your favor, but the mere threat of a *grievance,* also referred to as a "bluff," should not be a standard operating procedure. This is because your bluff can be called, and you may lose your *grievance* because it doesn't apply or is baseless to your claim. If your *grievance* makes its way to an arbitrator and the arbitrator disagrees with your position, the decision can have long lasting effects. And it is extremely difficult to gain back something you lost in a *grievance*. So, be careful to threaten an unwinnable *grievance* and do not file a *grievance* that cannot be won.

If you find yourself needing to get a win for your member and a formal *grievance* isn't appropriate, try a different route. Remember *Article 1.1*? Think about how a unified group of workers can force the company's hands to tilt a decision in your member's favor. Does your unified work force have leverage? And do you think you might get better results by using this leverage? If so, you could get a win without the threat of something you know you'll lose. No *grievance* filed, no court case, no arbitrator; just results delivered for your members by your members, using the strength of unity.

Filing a *grievance* is an exemplary tool in your tool bag, but you should not abuse the power a *grievance* carries.

3.2 - Making Your Members Whole

The idea of making a member "whole" is to ensure they receive everything they're entitled to as if they had never been violated in the first place. It's really that simple.

If a member was denied something they're clearly outlined to receive and you file a *grievance,* what all might the remedy entail? Even if the dispute is over something simple, are you 100% sure you could list every single item they're owed? Maybe you can, but to cover yourself and to deliver for your member, you'll want to include a remedy pursuing something to the effect of *"making your member whole in all ways"* because that gives you the ability to keep bringing up losses during negotiations.

Example: A pay dispute can impact more than lost wages. It can also impact retirement deposits, company savings programs, taxes specific to the employee, as well as anything else covered in your contract, such as shift scheduling or company specific perks.

If you think about delivering a result for your member and are unsure as to what all they're entitled to, using vague language will make it more feasible to get them everything they deserve. Think of it as an open-ended demand where you can essentially continue to pile on demands. Now, this doesn't necessarily mean you can demand things that your member isn't entitled to, and you shouldn't assume you can ask for more than what they're owed, but you can try to gain additional items from your employer—that is how you over deliver for a member, and that is a unifying delivery worth bragging about.

3.3 – Past Practices

When referring to past practices, what you're leaning on is a doctrine that has evolved over the years by union organizations, labor lawyers and arbitrators who've been assigned to interpret collective bargaining agreements when there's a disagreement between the two parties. A past practice is recognized as "a long standing, and undocumented practice that's been historically accepted and known to both the workers and management." To be considered a past practice, the practice must have been recognized for a reasonably long time, consistently applied on a frequent basis, and is both known and accepted by the union and the employer.

Sometimes a past practice is based on unspecific contract language, and other times it's as simple as an action the company has participated in with their employees for years.

Example: The contract lists specific unworked, paid holidays as well as language that says, "the company will endeavor to recognize additional holidays for special events," and for the last ten years the company has recognized all workers' birthdays as an unworked, paid holiday and has extended this practice to allowing workers to take a day off during the workweek if their birthday falls on a weekend. Then, abruptly, a new manager decides to stop recognizing this practice entirely.

A past practice cannot be taken away or changed without negotiating with the union first and can be grieved if the company abruptly chooses to no longer recognize the practice. A successful union steward will recognize past practices and argue on the behalf of the practice in the event the company wishes to stop the practice without negotiating with the union.

3.4 - Including But Not Limited To

Thus far, you've read the phrase "including, but not limited to," multiple times. Do you know what it means and how you can benefit from using language such as this? It is somewhat of irregular language written by lawyers, but it helps you in the event you need to file a *grievance*.

Whenever you file a *grievance*, you'll need to argue how the violation is in fact a violation. Was it a contractual obligation that your employer skipped out on? Did your boss violate a local, state, and/or federal law? Is the *grievance* a combination of many factors? Even if you're positive you know what the violation is, you're better off listing the violation as "including, but not limited to, [the known offense]" as the violation. This gives you the ability to make additional, and possibly wide-ranging arguments to achieve a positive outcome.

During a *grievance* procedure, you can expect your company to make up any argument they can to prove themselves correct and that they were/are within their legal boundaries to have run their business as they see fit, and you'll corner yourself by limiting your *grievance* to a single violation. So, don't limit yourself, and instead, broaden your scope to increase the chances you deliver a positive result for your members.

3.5 - The Seven Steps of Just Cause

The seven steps of "just cause" is a common standard in labor law and arbitration and is the designated method used in many union contracts to enforce job security. Simply put, "just cause" requires the employer to prove a member compromised the company in a specific way or acted in bad judgment by violating stated policies, laws, rules or regulations, and any disciplinary actions against said member are justified per the company policy and/or documented agreement with your union.

You can access variations of these steps online, but here is a rough synopsis of the steps with supporting information:

1. **The employee was fully aware of the company policy.**
   - **a)** Was the employee provided training or a learning opportunity and made fully aware of the stated policy, and the repercussions of violating such policy?
   - **b)** The policy must be available, clearly stated, unambiguous, and include the repercussions for violating said policy.
2. **The policy is reasonable.**
   - **a)** The policy must not be arbitrary, capricious, or discriminatory and must be related to the company's stated missions or objectives.
   - **b)** Employees are expected to follow company policy, but exceptions can be made in the event the policy jeopardizes the safety or health of the employee or others.
3. **Did the employer perform an investigation?**
   - **a)** Was there an investigation at all?
   - **b)** The employer is obligated to collect any and all facts pertaining to a relevant and final decision.
4. **Was the investigation fair and objective?**
   - **a)** The employer must perform a timely and thorough investigation while respecting the employees' rights.
   - **b)** All decisions must be free of bias or a preconceived conclusion.
5. **Is there substantial evidence of a clear policy violation?**
   - **a)** Did the investigation disclose proof or evidence the employee was guilty of violating or disobeying the rules or order?
   - **b)** Proof or evidence must be truly substantial but is not required to be beyond a reasonable doubt.
   - **c)** The company investigation must include a search for evidence that may clear the employee of wrongdoing.
   - **d)** If no offense can be proven, then no action should be taken as it is not considered as just.
6. **The policy is and has been consistently applied.**

a) Did the employer apply all rules and penalties for violations equally, without discrimination to all employees?

b) Have other employees guilty of the same violation been treated differently?

7. **The discipline was reasonable and appropriate.**

a) Was the level of discipline administered reasonably as it pertains to the seriousness of the employee's offense or historical record of past service?

b) A proven offense does not merit a harsh discipline unless the employee has been proven guilty of the same offense or similar offenses several time in the past.

c) In the event two employees are found guilty of the same offense, their individual records can and should be used to determine their individual discipline.

d) The employer has the right to issue a lesser or more severe penalty to an individual whose record is or isn't full of prior violations.

The seven steps of just cause are a treasure chest of opportunities for you to overturn unjust discipline. And a successful union steward will make compelling arguments referencing these seven steps when presenting a case against your employer, in front of an arbitrator or in any other legal proceeding.

3.6 - Protective Status

Under the framework of the National Labor Relations Act (the Federal labor law governing most American workers), and in many union contracts are protective statuses covering the role of a union steward. These protections apply whenever a steward is engaged in representative activities and places you on equal footing with management. While viewed as being on equal footing it is acceptable for you to behave in conduct that may otherwise be viewed as intolerable to your employer if you were not engaging in a representational manner. A union steward cannot be reprimanded for acting in their representative roles. I.e., you cannot be punished by your employer for filing grievances or for arguing with your boss over a perceived contract violation, etc. And your employer cannot overly supervise you or deny you the same opportunities, benefits, etc., as anyone else solely because of your status as a steward.

The many protections a union steward has stem from decisions made by the National Labor Relations Board. These decisions created broadly accepted rules, known as the "Equality Principle," "No Reprisals," and "Equal Standards," and they've established long-withstanding precedents protecting a steward's language and behavior.

To better understand the protections you have, read your contract and any other agreements between your union and employer, and research the applicable National Labor Relations Board decisions. If you feel your rights as a steward have been violated, you could have reason to file an unfair labor practice against your employer.

A steward's protected status does not permit you to blatantly ignore company policies or procedures or engage in illegal, outrageous, or indefensible conduct or behavior. So, utilize your powers and protections wisely when you're in a representative role and stay laser-focused on delivering for your members.

Article 3 - Scenario

Section 7 of your contract states that the employer must provide all employees working any given 9 hour shift an uninterrupted 45-minute lunch break, consisting of 30 minutes unpaid and 15 minutes of normal paid time. Recently, a manager started asking a member about details pertaining to a work-related topic 20 minutes into their lunch break. After your member informed the manager they had violated their contractual lunch break agreement, the manager stormed off threatening to reprimand the member for a minor violation of company policy taking place months ago, after the manager had originally deemed the minor violation a non-issue.

How would you address this scenario?

You could file a *grievance* with a selective focus on Section 7 of your union contract, but by doing so, you can leave arguing opportunities on the table because this scenario may contain local, state, or federal laws or legal stature violations, as well as possible retaliatory behavior that may work in your favor.

Do you see how a broader approach can give you more opportunities to argue on your member's case, and how a narrow focus could limit the success of your case?

Article Three Summary

A successful union steward understands their legal protections, can relate a member's case to legal precedents, and knows whether or not a formal _griev-ance_ is the best avenue to take when correcting an action or inaction taken against a member or group of members.

Representative activities place a steward on equal footing with management.
Never proceed with a "bluff" grievance.
Know your contract.
Deliver for your members.

grievance: noun – _a real or imagined wrong or other cause for complaint or protest, especially unfair treatment._

Notes: ____

____

____

____

____

____

____

Article Four

Investigations And Documentation

Successful union stewards quickly learn performing their own investigation, and detailed documentation is essential, especially in a heated arbitration. This is because arbitrators will often, but not always, look to notes and data collected from a steward when determining the legitimacy of a grievance, and may even make a decision based on the same information, or lack thereof. Among many other items, emails and communications between members, company leaders, and union officials can factor into arbitrational decisions. The better documentation a steward has of a scenario, the better chances that steward will help move the arbitration in your union's favor.

4.1 – Perform Your Own Investigation

Whenever your employer deems it's necessary to punish a member, they must perform a thorough investigation. *Article 3.4* explained what the company must do to prove guilt, but what can you as a steward do to prove innocence? Performing your own independent investigation is exactly how you prove a member's innocence. Your investigation is just that, it's your investigation. You are not limited to anything other than indefensible actions or coercion.

So, start by asking your members if they were witness to specific events and collect their statements as they apply to your investigation. If applicable, review company files, formal training, and all other documented records you have access to or can formally request from your employer. Review contract language, past grievances, and any applicable laws; then contact other stewards or union officials to ask for historical references you can lean on in order to build a refuting case against your employer.

One of the most important things a steward should investigate is the company policy, rule, or procedure they're claiming a member failed to comply with. Try to refute their decision by comparing the company's expectations to what they're claiming the member did or didn't do, and how the situation is reflective in your investigation notes. You should do this because companies may often make assumptions or will be quick to wrongfully accuse a member without linking them to an actual documented violation and that gives you an opportunity to dispute the accusation.

A pivotal point in your investigation should include you seeking out the truth from your member. This can be a difficult task because it's common for people to lie whenever they feel their livelihood is in jeopardy, and a member may instinctively lie to you. But if you don't understand the truth, even if it's incriminating, you will have a very difficult time protecting your member. So, ask your member to tell you the truth so you can do everything in your power to help them. Remember the lesson in *Article 1.2,* where your members must trust you? It should be much easier for them to tell you the truth if you've already gained their trust.

4.2 – The 'E' In E-Mail

What does email mean? Electronic mail, yes. But what does it translate to? Evidence. Evidence based mail. Everything in email format can, and many times will, last a lifetime. Most companies have an internal employee e-mail system for all to use. Some companies communicate directly via email, and sometimes you have to deal with customers, outside agencies or internal departments in email format. An email system can be your best friend and your worst enemy because an email has the essentials to a well-documented conversation; date, time, topic, and the names of everyone involved are clearly listed in an email. So, think about how specific data in an email is permanent and use it wisely.

When writing or responding via e-mail, be as accurate and articulate as you can whenever dealing in any representative communications. Just as in *Article 2.1*, you must show respect to earn respect, and by doing so, you're more likely to prevail when you communicate in an email, just as you would if you were in person. Don't let your emotions get the best of an important conversation. Being passive aggressive, disrespectful, and using an excessive amount of exclamation points to get a point across is more likely to fail than it is to help your members. Remember, you work for your members, and your communications will directly correlate to the outcomes you provide for them and the issues you're addressing.

4.3 – Who, What, When, Where, Why And How?

Think about the detailed notes a stenographer takes when documenting a court case. They're typing faster than most people think and if asked, they could reference very important information at the drop of a dime. This is because the detailed notes in court cases are objectively important to ensuring justice prevails. Additionally, a stenographer will *document* reactive body language, facial expressions, and other non-verbal forms of communication to ensure the entire process is captured in story format. A successful union steward will *document* as a stenographer would by taking detailed notes of events, meetings, interviews, and anything else pertinent to your workplace. When you *document* an event, *document* it as if your members' livelihoods depend on it because one day, they just might.

When documenting, there's no such thing as too much information to help you remember the facts of the event, and to assist you in painting a picture for whomever you'll need to explain the situation to at a later date. A successful steward will make their own note taking template and will carry a notebook, computer, tablet, or any other note taking device on hand whenever representing a member or having a detailed conversation with a company representative. It is truly essential for a steward to take detailed and situational notes in all representative activities.

Example: Today, I sat in with member Nicole and manager Amy to discuss the possibility of a temporary scheduling change as it relates to a childcare event that has taken place with Nicole. Nicole, to my left, is wearing her usual uniform and Amy, sitting across from me, has a new blue dress on taking hand written notes. The meeting started at approximately 2pm and is scheduled for 30 minutes in a company provided meeting room titled Meeting Room #3. During this meeting, Amy is engaged to Nicole's request to change the next 3 weeks of shift times, as outlined in the contract, in order to make lifestyle changes related to childcare. At 2:13pm, Nicole expressed a dire need for the temporary schedule change because the location her children are cared for is closing for renovations and her alternative childcare option is only available from 9am until 6:30pm. The change is only for 3 weeks and would start from beginning of shift time August 1st, through the end of shift August 22nd; starting no earlier than 9:30am and leaving no later than 6pm. Amy is understanding of the issue at hand and at 2:19pm says: "Nicole, you're a great team player and I will do everything I can to help you change your shift for the 3 weeks. Can you commit to working an additional day during the week, working 6 days, instead of 5 to help accommodate?" To this request, Nicole replies "Yes," and Amy states, "We have a deal, you'll start August 1st at 9:30am." We all leave the meeting in good standing, and Amy will send a confirmation of schedule changes to everyone by the end of the day. The time is 2:31pm and the meeting has ended with us leaving Amy to herself in the meeting room.

Can you see how detailed information could be helpful at a later date if anything is called into question?

Not all notes will be necessary to have at a later date, but you should <u>*document*</u> everything and keep them for as long as humanly possible. You never know what you'll need until you need it, and it's better to have things you don't need than to need things you don't have.

What else do you think you should <u>*document?*</u> The answer will be different based on the environment you work in but attempt to <u>*document*</u> conversations verbatim with a focus on key words from each individual and the time they spoke, plus include things like:

The meeting location.

Date. Time.

Names and roles of all in meeting attendance.

The color and style clothing they are wearing.

Questions and answers from all attendees.

Attendees' overall emotions.

Did anyone else take notes?

Was the need for the meeting clearly explained to all attendees?

Does your member know why they're in this meeting?

Does anyone need disability assistance or require medical attention?

Was any evidence discussed or presented?

Was the potential for discipline discussed?

Is a computer or other form of electronic recording device in use during this meeting?

Is the conversation being recorded?

Think about that last question…"Is this conversation being recorded?" is a great question for you to ask when you're in a representational meeting for many reasons. One reason is because it's legal in some states for single-party-consent to record a conversation and you might not be the single-party consenting to the conversation being recorded. Another reason you'd want to know if the conversation is being recorded is so you can assess how your communication would be viewed from a third party, in the event the conversation is played out loud for judgment's sake. Will your communications help or derail a subjective grievance? Remember *Article 3* and be fully aware of both your own individual legal rights, as well as the rights of, say, the human resources team, legal department, or management as a whole—just because you may get away with using abrasive language doesn't necessarily mean you need to or should. And if the conversation is recorded, how might your language be used against you or your members?

4.4 – Hidden Reasons

During an interview or meeting, a manager or human resources person may say the "quiet part out loud" or let the real reason slip for why they're interested in reprimanding a member of yours when attempting to reprimand them for something else. If this occurs, ask them to repeat themselves and *document* that you asked them to repeat it. If you're not alone, verify with other witnesses if they too heard what was said. *Document* their acknowledgment and ask them to make their own individual documentations as well. This can be important in the event you're grieving over a disciplinary action that isn't justified and need to call upon witness statements to substantiate your argument. Just as *Article 3.4* explained the seven steps of just cause, being wrongfully disciplined because the company failed to properly administer discipline, you might have the leverage you need to overturn the disciplinary action taken. So, _document_ everything you can and combine statements from other witnesses to build a stronger case.

One thing to keep in mind is, as important as witness statements are, they're not absolute in pursuing a preferred outcome for your grieving member or members. Just as in _Article 4.1_ you must complete your own investigation and find other forms of proof to combine with the witness statements. Successful union stewards actively seek witness statements because this helps them solidify a narrative, but a successful union steward will also search for other supporting information in the event witness statements are not enough to win their case.

There will come a time where you'll have to make a judgment call and decipher if your member is about to be justifiably reprimanded but will be given a lighter level of discipline than what is historically called for. This can be a tough situation to be in because your job is to demand fairness on the job and equal treatment, right? Now on one hand, you as a steward cannot and should not request or negotiate more harsh discipline for a member, and on the other hand, you can probably link this members' scenario to a previous incident and recognize the differences aren't fair. So, what do you do? Do you let the current situation go as planned and then try to use it as a building block to lessen future disciplinary actions taken against your members? Are there contributing factors, such as a protected status, etc., you should evaluate? Will you file a grievance for the previous disciplinary actions taken against your members because the company is unevenly asserting discipline? And if so, do you think that's a grievance you'll win? There's no specific right or wrong answer in these situations because each situation will be unique to itself. But a successful union steward can evaluate all angles of information and turn an event like this as a tool... A tool to add to your tool bag that you can later reach for to further help your members.

Article 4 – Scenario

While working, you and two members overhear a pair of supervisors discussing another member's job performance, and one supervisor mentions a uniquely specific medical condition as a reason for their performance. At this time, the other supervisor acknowledges the member's "poor" performance is *due to their condition but stressed that the employer is not allowed to discipline the member because of their protected status and disclosed medical condition. Instead, they decide to "hunt" for other reasons to discipline and terminate the member so they can "hire a better and healthier employee."*

If you and two members overhear this conversation, what do you think would be important information to *document* amongst yourselves so you can be ready to defend your member? And do you think a time and dated e-mail or text message might end up benefiting your case more than hand written notes?

During this event, do you notice if there are any identifying markers, such as unique clothing the supervisors are wearing or if they're standing within observation of a surveillance camera you should take note of? And if so, do you think this might help you later?

Article Four Summary

A union steward's best friend is their own note taking and proof of documentation. Learning how and when the best time to use electronic documentation vs. handwritten notes is key in both documenting a story and keeping the company unaware of your actions. A successful union steward will perform their own investigation and use all available tools as an advantage to win cases for their members.

Document everything.

Deliver for your members.

document: noun – a piece of written, printed, or electronic matter that provides information or evidence or that serves as official record.

Notes: ____

____

____

____

____

____

____

Article Five

References And Resources

No matter what industry you work in, your _labor_ is directly impacted by decisions made from laws, rules, and regulations. While many American workers have additional benefits based on the state they live in, most benefit from many Federal laws designed to promote the health and safety in the workforce, as well as protections from corruption within union leadership and unlawful actions from an employer. Additionally, there are some laws that hinder or complicate workplace union activities.

A successful union steward would review the following and study how they apply to themselves and their members:

5.1 – Weingarten Rights

NLRB v. J. Weingarten 1975

Landmark United States Supreme Court decision upholding an important decision made by the National _Labor_ Relations Board (NLRB) declaring a union represented employee has the right to union representation during an investigatory interview. Most commonly referred to as your Weingarten Rights.

If an employee makes a clear request for union representation prior to or during an interview, the company must grant the request in one of three ways:

1. Delay any further questioning until the representative arrives and has had a chance to speak privately with the member.
2. Offer the member a chance to proceed without representation.
3. End the interview.

It would be an unfair *labor* practice if the company does not follow one of their three options, and a member can refuse to answer any further questioning.

5.2 – Laws Pertaining To Labor

Below is list of laws with a brief synopsis of how they pertain to *labor*. Though many of these laws also include other topics and rights, this list outlines how they benefit you and your members on the job. You can also lean on these laws, as well as any proceeding court cases related to the law in a grievance or arbitration case.

As you learned in *Article 2.4*, your personal beliefs about individual laws are not as important as your responsibility to represent your members' interests. So, regardless of how you may feel, you should utilize these laws as necessary.

Independent research is highly encouraged to enhance your understanding of the following:

Civil Rights Act of 1866

Affirms all U.S. citizens are equally protected under the laws of the United States and makes it illegal to deny a person citizenship based on their race or color. Wasn't initially written as a *labor* law, but later was amended to support civil rights within *labor*.

National Railway *Labor* Act of 1926

Applies mostly to railroad and airline workers. Limits *labor* unrest, i.e., striking, so that the nation's main routes of transportation and commerce are not impacted. Additionally, the law established a pathway for workers to "grieve" issues through federal court, instead of the more common form of arbitration.

Norris-LaGuardia Act of 1932

Written to protect workers right to organize, picket, and strike by preventing the courts from intervening at the behest of the employer. Prior to the law, courts would issue injunctions against workers who picket, organized, or went on strike, and many were fined if they persisted.

National *Labor* Relations Act of 1935

Nation's first private sector *labor* law "with teeth" protecting workers right to concerted activities, the right to organize, to go on strike, and to bargain for better working conditions. Established the National *Labor* Relations Board made up of presidentially appointed members overseeing violations filed by workers against their employer for violations of the law. Such violations must be filed within a six-month time period from the date of accused violation. Most private sector workers are covered under this act. It is considered an unfair *labor* practice if an employer or *labor* union violates the act.

Fair *Labor* Standards Act of 1938

Sets a federal minimum wage requirement, prohibits child *labor*, and standardized the eight-hour work day, and overtime pay. Before this law, and due to their smaller size, many children died as a result of being forced to work difficult jobs where an adult wouldn't fit, i.e., tight spaces in large machinery and mechanical enclaves.

Taft-Hartley Act of 1947

A series of amendments to the landmark NLRA of 1935, preventing a worker from picketing another worker's employer, and allows the passage of state "right to work" laws, allowing workers to opt out of being required to join a union at their workplace.

Labor Management Reporting And Disclosure Act of 1959

Designed to prevent racketeering and corruption within a *labor* management relations. Requires *labor* unions to adopt democratic processes to elect union officials, giving each union member a voice in the process.

The Equal Pay Act of 1963

Makes it illegal to pay men and women differently for performing the same work in the same workplace.

Title 7 of The Civil Rights Act of 1964

Amendment made to the 1866 *Civil Rights Act* to protect workers from being denied job opportunities, wages and other compensations of employment based solely on the worker's race, color, religion, sex, or national origin.

Age Discrimination in Employment Act of 1967

Prohibits discrimination against people over the age of 40 and prohibits both employers and unions from excluding workers over the age of 40.

Occupational Safety and Health Act of 1970

Requires employers to keep their workplace safe from hazardous conditions. Under this law, employers are required to inform and train their employees of all dangers related to their work, provides workers a route to file a complaint about workplace safety, and protects workers from employer retaliation for filing a complaint over safety concerns.

Worker Adjustment And Retraining Notification Act of 1988

Gives employees who'll be subject to a plant closure or mass layoffs time to prepare and react to their loss of employment by being issued a 60-day WARN notice. Must be followed by employers with over 100 permanent headcount and applies to hourly and salaried workers, including management and supervisory roles. Few exemptions are allowed to forgo the 60-day notice requirements, including natural disasters and unforeseen business circumstances.

Family Medical Leave Act of 1993

Allows eligible workers to take specific amount of time off, up to twelve weeks, without pay from work without fear of losing their employment or employer sponsored medical coverage after reaching minimum tenure of one year and requires workers to have worked a minimum number of hours that years' time before they're eligible to benefit from the act. Employers can offer eligibility to employees prematurely to reaching the laws' stated tenure and hours if they so choose, but they're not obligated to.

5.3 - Government Organizations

In relation to the laws listed in *Article 5.2*, there are government agencies who enforce their requirements. The nature of the violations you're experiencing will determine which agency you would contact, or the act that you would reference in a grievance. It's important you know who to contact based on what services they provide.

Example: A situation where your employer increased pay for all workers except a select group of people whose skin color is different isn't necessarily a workplace safety issue but it's definitely a violation of workers' rights.

Government agencies and a brief synopsis of what they do:

Department of *Labor* (DOL) – *dol.gov*

Core worker governing department under the Executive Branch of the Federal Government. Its current form was established in 1913 after many years of structural, operational and name changes. The agency is responsible for administering federal laws as they pertain to *labor*, and to foster, promote, and develop the welfare of wage earners, job seekers, and retirees. They also strive to improve working conditions, advance opportunities for profitable employment, and ensure worker benefits and rights are upheld.

National *Labor* Relations Board (NLRB) – *nlrb.gov*

An independent review board created out of the National *Labor* Relations Act safeguarding employees' rights to organize their workplace and conducts union elections, investigates charges filed by a worker, makes rules pertaining to the National *Labor* Relations Act language, and encourages disputes be settled without the need for litigation. The board is made of 32 regional offices spread across the United States. Each regional office is made of lawyers and agents who investigate complaints and setup union elections. Unfair *labor* practice violations can be filed with the NLRB and a charge may be bought against the employer if the board determines a violation occurred. Additionally, union members can file complaints against their union if they feel their union fails to represent them—highlighting the importance of a steward to not only document their interactions with their members but also to work closely with their union when representing a member or group of members.

<u>Occupational Safety and Health Administration (OSHA)</u> – *osha.gov*

Is a division of the Department of <u>*Labor*</u> (DOL) and their mission is to ensure safe and healthy working conditions for workers by setting and requiring standards by providing training, outreach, education, and assistance. Made up of ten regional branches throughout the United States. Employees are encouraged to contact OSHA whenever there's a workplace safety concern. OSHA, along with some individual states' programs will assign someone to inspect the concern and help the company develop a procedural practice to ensure the company remains compliant and the workers are safe. The department also ensures no worker will be retaliated against for contacting the agency over their perception of unsafe working conditions.

<u>U.S. Department of Veterans Affairs (VA)</u> – *va.gov*

A department dedicated to ensuring U.S. veterans are offered the care they need for anything from mental and physical conditions to education assistance, home loans and life insurance. An all-around resource for your military members, in the event they need assistance once they return to civilian life and the workforce.

5.4 - Non-Government Organizations

Along with the many departments of government you as a steward have to rely on, there are also many not-for-profit groups as well. Each one is a resource of itself, and many successful union stewards learn to reach out to a specific organization for help.

Not-for-profit groups and a brief synopsis of what they do:

<u>American Federation of *Labor* and Congress of Industrial Organizations (AVL-CIO)</u> – *aflcio.org*

A coalition of unions and union workers, and the largest affiliation of organized <u>*labor*</u> in the U.S. striving for better wages and working conditions for all

American workers, and many international workers. Partnering with nearly 60 recognized _labor_ unions, many community, constituency, and allied groups, state and federal _labor_ councils, and many trades associations across the U.S., they offer services including access to apprenticeships and training programs for workers to gain new skills needed for an ever-changing employment environment. Additionally, they give those seeking to unionize their workplace a confidant to work with and resources to help their organizing drive achieve success.

American Civil Liberties Union (ACLU) – _aclu.org_

Nearly 100-year-old non-profit and non-partisan organization made of lawyers and legal experts working to protect American liberties and often working on behalf of workers whose workplace rights, as well as individual rights, were violated during their employment.

Alcoholics Anonymous (AA) – _aa.org_

Founded in 1935 and has become an international aid fellowship program using a twelve-step program dedicated to promoting abstinence-based recovery from alcohol. They offer plenty of information a steward could use in the event they need to help a member in need.

National Alliance on Mental Illness (NAMI) – _nami.org_

Starting in 1979 as a "kitchen table group", is now a nationwide grassroots organization dedicated to helping all Americans impacted by mental illness live better lives. Working with over 600 affiliates and nearly 50 state organizations to bring awareness and resources to those who are struggling with their own personal mental illness or have a friend, family member or co-worker who suffers from mental illness.

American Foundation for Suicide Prevention (AFSP) – _afsp.org_

A foundation based on providing lifesaving access and educational help day or night. Offering learning segments so you can identify someone who might be struggling and offer them the help they deserve. They have community resources and support groups in thousands of cities and offer virtual assistance if the situation calls for it.

For emergent assistance:
- Call: 988
- Text: "TALK" to 741741
- Dial: 911 for suicidal emergencies

Article Five Summary

There are laws, and both government and non-government resources available for a union steward to utilize to gain more preferable outcomes for their members. A successful union steward knows the proper department to contact for their specific issues, the appropriate laws to reference when a violation has taken place, and the best resource group to contact to help save a member's life.

Utilize your legal resources.
Know how the law works for you and how the law works against you.
Deliver for your members

labor: noun – work, especially hard physical work.

Notes: ____

____

____

____

____

____

____

Article Six

Bargaining > Arguing

———————

As a steward, you'll learn that you often have to bargain for an arrangement or agreement between a member or a group of members and company bosses, and at times, between differing members. But how do you address a situation that isn't contractual or legally binding yet still requires your dedication to facilitate an agreement or decree? The answer will obviously vary based on the industry you work in, but these can be burdensome in any workplace if you're unable to help. And without your help, any small situation may escalate into something more serious.

Depending on the specifics, you'll need to address each situation differently but you can evaluate most situations similarly using the following method:

First, you'll need to find out who all is involved in the dispute.

Second, you need a full understanding of how everyone feels about the dispute, what their proposed solutions may be, and what compromises they might be willing to make to end the dispute.

Third, attempt to get all parties together to "hash out their differences." Give everyone the same opportunity to talk but set an expectation that everyone be respectful during the conversation.

Fourth, find common ground for people to agree on and direct the conversation for one another to emphasize what they agree on. If necessary, try to compartmentalize and sway people to disregard their subtle differences so everyone feels as if their primary points are recognized. You do this because people will often want a similar outcome but have varying ways of achieving it. So, unifying people on a bargained outcome is an ideal goal. If necessary, seek alternative options that might accommodate everyone's desired outcome, and ask everyone to agree to an end point.

Lastly, allow an appropriate amount of time to pass then check in with everyone after an agreement has been implemented and everyone has moved on with their normal activities.

There's no exact timeline to which you'll need to address disagreements but you'll want to show everyone that you're engaged and working for a solution. Remind everyone on an individual level that their concerns are important to you, and always redirect anger towards your employer, not one another.

6.1 – Member vs. Member

A member vs. member situation is a dividing mechanism many company bosses will use to pit workers against each other. Why? Because a divided group of workers is less likely to be organized enough to demand better when the time comes. So, do your best to keep the company unaware of member vs. member issues and work with everyone to come to an acceptable resolution.

Member vs. member situations often leave little room for you to bargain because no matter what the issue, one, if not all members involved may inevitably feel as if they lost something. But a successful union steward can make their members feel better about the final outcome. When possible, redirect all anger towards your employer. Is the reason why the members are fighting because management has placed too much pressure on everyone? Has the business made decisions that are having negative effects on these specific members or the membership as a whole? By turning the emotions against your employer and not one another, you can not only successfully bargain with your members, but you can also build further solidarity, just as was covered in *Article 1*.

When you intervene or bargain between two members, it's vital that you remain unattached or sided to one member's outcome over the other's and instead seek what's best for both members. You might agree or disagree with one individual, but your personal feelings need to remain irrelevant because you work for both members, and you don't want a single member feeling isolated or to perceive that you're siding against them.

Under no circumstance should you argue with a member, especially over a mundane issue. Just as *Article 1.2* stated the importance of trust your members have in you, you'll need to ensure that both members can trust their interests are important to you, even if you personally disagree.

Keep in mind that not all issues may rise to the same high level of significance, but any issue between members can cause turbulence among the rank and file.

Example: Two members are arguing over a parking spot and the argument begins to get heated. Being the steward, you intervene to get them to stop arguing and to propose a solution. During the discussion one member mentions the importance of the specific parking spot due to the shade provided by a tree nearest to the spot, and their need for this is because they like to take a nap in their car during break time. The other member claims the spot is available for anyone to use, as a first come, first served basis. After listening to both parties speak their side, you review the company handbook and read that there are no assigned parking spots for anyone other than security or people with disabilities.

Can you see how a situation like this can be both infuriating for your members and can be an opportunity for a company boss to drive a wedge between them? It might seem like a minimal issue, parking that is, but a successful union steward will keep issues like this away from the boss and bargain a preferred outcome for both members.

6.2 – Member vs. Manager

Inevitably, you'll have situations where a member and manager are disagreeing on assignments or simply not getting along with one another over issues you can't file a formal grievance against. So, how do you address these interactions? Remember in *Article 2* that you'll need to show you respect the manager if you have any chance of <u>*bargaining*</u> with them. And, just as you need to respect the manager, you'll need to deliver an ideal result for your member.

First and foremost, you must know if the member is in the right or in the wrong because your response will be defined by their actions.

If your member is in the right, then you'll want to make unified arguments and provide supplemental points to justify the member's reasoning. Try not arguing over the issue or issues, and instead leverage your unification to convince the manager they're standing on a hill that's not worth dying on. At times, you may need to cut a deal with the manager over an unrelated topic or redirect the ending of the conversation to a priority of the manager's so the manager feels as if they weren't completely steamrolled and can walk away with some remaining dignity. If you bargain a deal or allude to completing a specific task for the manager, make sure you uphold your end of the deal, then follow up with the manager once you've completed it. Doing this is referred to as positive reinforcement, and this reinforcement will open the door for you to continue _bargaining_ with the manager in the future.

If your member is in the wrong, you'll want to give the manager the feeling as though you agree with them but you'll need to push them to view things from the member's perspective. By convincing the manager to view the conversation differently, they might be willing to back off their position enough for you to find common ground and end the interaction in a more positive direction. If you're unable to convince the manager to view things differently, the conversation becomes further divisive or heated, or you assess that you're not going to come to any agreement, then resort to the lesson of *Article 2.4 – agree to disagree* and backpedal the conversation to something more positive or completely unrelated.

6.3 – Working To The Rule

Working to the rule is often spoken as "work-to-the-letter," and could be referred to as an "antithesis." It can be summed up as: fulfilling the absolute intent of a documented process or series of processes by doing the bare minimum exactly as it's expected without taking any shortcuts to improve time or efficiency by following all applicable rules, and safety regulations—all while withholding from doing anything extra.

Example: The company policy requires five employees on staff at the same time to jointly perform a certain set of tasks in alignment with a list of safety rules and regulations. Yet, this policy is routinely ignored because the company is usually understaffed and the amount of time it takes to complete the work and follow the policy takes away from other priorities. One day, after an employee is severely injured, the remaining workers withhold from completing the specific work until the employer hires and trains the sufficient number of work-

ers to safely complete the work per the employer's policy, and to remain in align-ment with all safety rules and regulations.

If this were to happen, do you think the work would be completed? And do you see how this has the potential to be a *bargaining* chip?

In order to get your members on board with this idea, you'll need to en-sure you have unity among them first. Just as *Article 1* stated, unity is your strongest power, and showing a force of power by working to the rule is a powerful way to bargain, especially if you have no other leverage to force your employer to the *bargaining* table.

One thing to keep in mind is if you work to the rule or are going to with-hold labor for safety reasons, that doesn't necessarily justify ignoring other work that can be safely performed. Being a successful union steward, you should be able to accurately recognize what is and is not pertinent to safety. Equally, you should be able to see what reasonable corners you and your members should and should not take to ensure you truly work to the rule.

Working to the rule is a powerful way to get attention to something that has negative impacts on your members, but you should always approach this tactic with extreme caution. If you're found to be misusing the tactic or your union organization is found to be practicing this in bad faith, then your union can be held legally accountable for your employers' financial losses if the losses are directly related to a slowdown of work.

Now, this doesn't mean you cannot address workplace safety issues as necessary; this simply means you may be required to justify your actions in a potential legal setting. A successful union steward will recognize all risks as-sociated from all potential outcomes of their decisions before following through with any action to address work-place safety concerns.

As listed in *Article 5.3*, the Occupational Safety and Health Administration (OSHA) is a great resource for a steward to contact when evaluating a safety concern. And you should thoroughly communicate with you union organiza-tion before making any decisions on your own.

Just as *Article 1.1* covered that you cannot and should not coerce anyone to participate in moments of solidarity, you equally cannot and should not co-erce anyone to work to the rule or withhold their labor for safety concerns. Notwithstanding, unity is your strongest power.

Article Six Summary

Spending less time being combative and focusing on *bargaining* for balanced and acceptable outcomes for your members should remain a priority and objective of a successful union steward.

Never pick sides between members.
Leverage unity to force your employer to bargain.
Find common ground.
Deliver for your members.

bargaining: verb – the act of, negotiating the terms and conditions of a transaction.

Notes: _______________________________________

____

____

____

____

____

In Closing

Thus far, you should have noticed a theme of this book focusing on your behavior as a steward, and the importance of your behavior as it directly relates to the successes you can achieve being a dedicated steward.

To reference a familiar quote, you will achieve more if you offer someone honey than you would if you were to offer them vinegar. And this is especially true when you're viewed as the person who will literally protect people's livelihoods.

The role of a union steward is not always black and white, and it often fades between the lines of these two viewed points. You'll be a successful union steward whenever you begin to see the paths between the lines of correct and incorrect, the difference between doing things the right way and doing things the wrong way, and the difference between the correct way of doing things the right way and the correct way of doing things the wrong way; and when you can successfully direct your members towards the appropriate path they should follow.

You may or may not know it at first, but you are the backbone of the current labor movement. You are dedicating yourself to stand willing and eager to defend the rights of your members and all workers everywhere. You bring justice to those who have been wronged by their employer. And, you are a light at the end of a tunnel, for some who are suffering.

Yes, you deserve more praise than you'll ever receive, but then again, you're not doing this for the glory—you're doing this because it's difficult, because it's the work that no one else will do, because you're the right person for the right reasons, and because you believe an injustice to one is an injustice to all.

Your success is dependent on your dedication to your members, and your ability to motivate them to dedicate themselves to their union.

So, with additional resources, and a newly refined "tool bag" for you to become a successful union steward....

Are you ready?